T0198851

Secrets Within

Nadine Rhymer

authorHOUSE®

AuthorHouse™
1663 Liberty Drive
Bloomington, IN 47403
www.authorhouse.com
Phone: 1 (800) 839-8640

Published by AuthorHouse   11/07/2016

ISBN: 978-1-5246-4947-0 (sc)
ISBN: 978-1-5246-4946-3 (e)

Print information available on the last page.

This book is printed on acid-free paper.

Secrets—to have knowledge of something that is kept or meant to be kept unknown or

Un seen by others. Hidden, underground mysterious.

Abuse—A bad effect or for a bad purpose; misuse. treating a person or animal with cruelty

Or violence, especially regularly or repeatedly by, the improper use of something.

Assault—to mistreat someone especially a woman or a child sexually.

Use or treat in such a way as to cause damage or harm—insults, to be rude, swear at, curse, call someone names, taunt, shout at slander.

This is a topic that touches me personally! Mainly because at 44 years old I am just now at the age where I can actually honestly say that I love ME! Ever since I was little, as far back as 3 years old, I remember feeling ugly and not lovable. Now the question is what would make a 3 year old feel ugly and unloved? Well its simple I was shown through abuse and having to live every day with a secret that consumed my soul and robbed me of any and all happy feelings I could have ever felt. It has been known that most victims that don't get help such as counseling and deep therapy; they tend to carry down certain behaviors. So on and so on. I have siblings who have shown similar emotional damage and have carried on the taught behavior onto those in their presence. Their children and spouses or friends, I have to sadly say that I am also guilty for showing and acting out certain behaviors. Such as speaking badly about others, or acting spiteful, hateful towards others simply because I was so sad and hurting inside. Always feeling suspicious of what others are truly saying of feeling about me. Never feeling good enough or pretty enough.

Always seeking approval and acceptances. When looking in the mirror never seeing anything but ugly. All through school I remember always being in trouble. I can say it was because I was never getting the proper attention which eventually became negative attention for not behaving and for disrupting. It carried on all through my school years. I could never seem to keep friends mainly because I could never really let anyone close or let my guard down. When you are a victim of sexual abuse you have severe trust issues, always suspicious of people's motives. Scared of being hurt, therefore using the strongest defense mechanism. The Wall.

With me my wall was so big and so strong, King Kong could not have made it through. Living with such a strong handicap of low self—esteem, which caused me to become one who never lost any fight or obstacle that arose, I would have conquered just to not fail. The worst part living in such darkness is that in my younger years especially at the time it took place, it was so shamed upon that no one dared tell anyone that I was being abused, especially my father, mainly because he was such an intense man, He was always yelling and threatening. Not that he would have punished me, but the not sure of what he would do was what kept me from feeling I could tell him. As I got older and the abuse continued

I started realizing that I would seek inappropriate attention. I learned at such a young age that the only way I felt loved was to give love (sex). I became sexually active of my own consent as young as 12 1/2 years old. I felt actually I was acting out, like I was turning the tables. Now I was in control, as though I thought.

Because it was my choice, not theirs. I matured quickly, I was extremely tall for my age, at 13 years old I looked 16 or older mentally and stood 6'0 feet tall. So yes I looked older than I was, and because I carried myself well. And with this terrible secret I would just sit with the adults and listen to adult conversation, it made me wise beyond my years. That's why people should really filter their conversations and actions in front of young children because they learn fast!

They hear things that strike their curiosity, which then causes them to seek answers or experiment with other kids their own age..

In the 70s and 80s I realize that child sexual abuse existed more than it was spoken about, and that's because of a number of reasons. It was "hush hush" and I remember hearing comments that the child was to blame. That they were the wrong ones, they were bad. That mentality still exists to this day. People say she or he shouldn't have brought such attention to themselves, or if it took place while she or he was under the influence, then they asked for it. The most common one is because of their choices in clothes how they were dressed. I also hear "well she was a slut or a whore". LET ME SAY ONE THING! Listen very closely! Nothing excuses the act of rape or sexual abuse against a child or young adolescent or women . . . .

This has become a topic that passes through the inked newspapers articles or social media CNN reports. It seems that it no longer fazes anyone. In fact I feel they are more focused on how many likes or views they received on their provocative for thousands of men, single, married, underage to distract and consume their sexual hunger. This epidemic flood of dysfunction of exposing flesh over the world wide web that has opened a door of diseased world revolved around un holy acts of lusts. Feeding abusive behavior, Divorce is at an all time high, Romance has turned into speed hook ups not even dating. Children are becoming sexually active earlier than they can even comprehend, babies having babies. Less and less love, more and more cold unattached, emotionless relationships. More hatred due to broken hearts, broken souls. Some take a shot to the heart so painful that it permenately damages them. They become bitter, dark, lifeless inside. I believe that if we as a whole don't stop and notice what's going on eventually love will no longer exists, would be like living without air. We would all cease to live.

Children who grow up in families without love never, learn how to love, If they never learn to love, they will never fall in love and never have babies and build strong family foundation, without families we then become ONE.

STANDING ALONE in this crazy, scary, destructive world.

We have learned to ignore and to medicate those who cannot seem to be able to bottle up their feelings and emotions. They are considered chemically unbalanced. A reference made by me when describing my mother a reference made about me numerous times, being a survivor of child abuse I can see the signs of others who have suffered the same or even worse. My heart bleeds for them. You will find generally not factually that the majority of abused children grow up to be extremely eager to please others, sexually or by anyway they feel they will achieve approval. Some become very successful, because they build such a barrier around them and knock down anything that stands in their way. They fight to survive and tell you only what they feel safe sharing. And literally live a life of lies, behavior brought on from such a young age. Because they were never able to share the truth. Sometimes they create this life that is not at all close to reality yet almost becomes or seems like a reality to them. Sometimes from sharing it so much they begin to believe it themselves, and the energy of success starts there.

That's how some of the most creative possession's become songs, paintings, books, pictures etc. Talents that can be stolen from someone from someone who has survived, because even they may have survived which is a miracle in its self, but without positive influence to help them believe in themselves. I have had a few great ones who stood by me and showed me what they saw in me something that I never seen in myself Always lifting me up never putting me down for the mistakes that I have made, allowing me to see that even though I was not proud of my mistakes that did not define me.

Time eventually erases all mistakes made, I am a firm believer that people do change, it just takes longer time to earn trust from those they have hurt. The old saying is "once a liar always a liar" or once a thief always a thief". I one truly wants to prove themselves they must show consistent positive improvement and back up their words – Proof is in the pudding.

See as a survivor of sexual abuse anyone we meet could be one or the other, liars or thieves that is. Simply because we were lied to and robbed of our most precious possessions (our innocence). something we can never take back once gone. People who do such destroying actions don't realize what they are taking.

Let me be clear about a few things. Child sex abuse – people think of pedophiles. One who preys on small kids at a playground in a school yard hiding out in a shady looking van trying to lure kids with candy or a puppy. That is now considered as a stereo type these days. Now its likely to exists 1 out of every 5 homes or even more. I haven't done the statistics but I do see the red dots on the map or registered sexual offenders. That says enough for me. So with that said, anything said or done in a inappropriate manner with sexual intent is what I am concerned about. We have lost all control to discipline our children, the control to determine how to dress, where to go and who they hang around. The worst I have found is Social Media, it cause gone out of control, so much that it is now being used to advertise prostitution and sex trafficking underage soliciting. There are drugs now that literally alters the mind so much that while these acts are taking place it keeps anyone from reacting and stopping those terrible actions.

Sometimes we may be in an abusive relationship and it may not seem like it, we usually can identify the common abusive relationship, the kind that involves control, name calling and physical abuse. Another kind of abuse is the kind that deceit in the main factor, where one is being led to believe that they are the only one in their partners life, yet that not at all being the truth. Lies being told to cover up their actions, lack of receiving love from the one who is deceiving, because they are not capable of giving all their love when you are giving love to more than one person, there's never enough to go around. and usually the one being deceived is so frustrated that they stop showing love towards the one who is hurting them.

Then there is sexual abuse that exists even in a marriage treating the wife with disrespect, calling her names in bed like she is a bad girl, whore or slut. Please forgive my direct examples. But women have been steered to think that this is ok. Some women do not tolerate it. But there are some that are lacking in self-esteem and feel that feel that if they say anything then the men won't want to be with them. God bless those strong women. I have been that insecure girl lacking in self-esteem and the strong one that would put an end to the kind of that behavior. In the beginning the relationship is exciting and new but after the new wears off and the arguments begin, the woman doesn't find it so exciting anymore. From my experience and from what I have heard from we have just forgotten about our self—worth. Society has lost total control on the morals of dating, the age exposure is younger and younger, Girls look older than they should because of the growth hormones and dress completely inappropriate, showing too much skin and we no longer try to control it. Then with the uncontrolled traffic of drugs, teens are losing sight of how to say no to inappropriate behavior, and because its so hard to fit in these days and the pressure just to be in the crowd.

Due to the lack of love in this world and the overpowering disease of narcissism no one cares anyone to prevent the bad behaviors.

I have heard and seen such awful, terrible behaviors and acts upon very young children, Ive heard of people literally forming groups or cults, where in these groups so much sexual activity takes place and I have read in other countries and cultures children as young as 7 months old.

It makes my heart bleed.

In order for girls and boys to love themselves they need not associate sex with love. I have always said that we need to stop reading fairytales to our daughters, we need to encourage them to be athletic or artistic, support them even when they want to give up. Tell them every day that they will succeed. When we are young we all read stories of fairytales, how your knight in shining armor will come along and kiss you and you will fall in love at first kiss. Instead we should read the bible to our kids teaching them from right and wrong, leading them to the love of Christ in their hearts not always waiting for the right one to come along. The bible tells us

God has a plan for all of us, we just need to have patience and faith. I was guilty of not having much patience nor was I taught the ways of the bible, therefore I have had numerous, endless lobe affairs. All were based on sex and that was brought on from the sexual abuse growing up.

Never allowing the good guys to get close, because of the abuse the good ones I was afraid of, because no one had ever showed me good. Nor did I ever let them get close enough to show me. So many times had I tried to pick the right one, but because the relationships were built on sex I was not showing myself respect and not demanded it from the men in my life, and from the years of abuse buried the seed of mistrust so deep that with every heart break or bad relationship added another brick to the wall that was built to protect me from getting hurt again. Always expecting a different outcome with every new relationship, I feel that if I had been brought up in church I feel that a lot of my heartache would have not existed, yet I often say I thank God for the journey he has taken me on, was so that I could truly work in his name and to help those overcome the struggle living as a survivor of sexual abuse, physical and mental abuse.

After years of trying it on my own and 3 marriages and countless break ups, I broke down and asked God for help. From that moment on my whole life changed, All the years of sadness and feeling unloved all went away truly went away. I spent three or four days taking with God and repenting all my sin's and asking him to heal me from all the pain I had endured as a young child and pain that I had brought upon myself as an adult by allowing others to treat me badly.

It was an amazing experience one that was so much of the Holy Spirit that no one would believe me if I were to try and explain. Every-day since then I grow closer to God and have been able to see myself through his eyes, love myself as he loves me and love others without judging or ill intentions. It has allowed me and empowered me to begin my mission with for God and help others who suffer with the same issues. I feel that I have the desire to take away the pain, fill it with happiness. I have been fortunate enough to have the will to rise above the pain, never truly allow myself to lose the battle and be defeated by grief.

I read the other day an article about a man takes his pregnant wife to the hospital to get a check u, he was fourty and he said she was 20, and that's not un heard of, it was because she was actually twelve years old. This took place in another country, out of the united states, I was so upset that I began to cry for this girl. When I was younger it was known of young girls being pregnant at the age of twelve, but it was not common and was a sad situation for the young girl, realizing that her childhood has come to an end, now a child is raising a baby. News reports being made all over the world of hundreds of young girls and boys being taken against their will, being made to have sex and make sexual films for money. never to be returned and even murdered. Those children will live in horror for the rest of their lives until someone fights for their lives.

Because of this behavior those kids will not grow up and have families and children of their own. Growing up as slaves, abused, tortured Never experiencing a quality life, I plan to build a foundation to help survivors of this kind of abuse, and nurture them back to happiness with the help of God's love.

Women truly need to come together and support each other and lift each other up, love each other, hold each other close and not take away from. Tell each other we are beautiful, listen to our fears, never lie to one another, bring back the wholesome in our hearts, and start molding mothers again. Those who have suffered abuse become some of the strongest people I have ever known.

Myself, I have seen a lot in my life, hard times and some really good times. Made many friends all over, in every state I have lived, I meet people and treat them as if I've known them for years. I never judge people on how much money they have or their possession's nor how much they don't have. I have had money and been poor throughout my life. I

27

realized at a very young age when you die you can't take it with you, and after you die it just becomes something the family members and friends fight over. Your name is all you can take with you.

I have met people throughout my life who have overcome such devastating times in their lives and they have all told me it was because they asked God to come into their hearts. Just as I have not too long ago. And I must truly say I wished I had known how wonderful it really is I would have opened my heart long before now. After I got saved I started truly seeing the sadness in others eyes. How we all are on a journey and everyone suffers from something. we lack in confidence and self—love. So someone, some-where someone has broken their spirit. And from that moment on their self-worth was never the same, never regained to the fullest.

With our society most don't stand a chance, always competing with what we have been programmed to think we should be.

Myself, love was always at all-time low until the day I had my heart broken for the last time by someone I put so much trust and effort into. I remember at that moment that I would never allow anyone to have control of my self—worth again. I began to truly love myself and THAT my friends is the greatest of all times. Especially when you have asked God into your heart, because then you feel the love he has for you. The best tool you can ever have is the tool of courage, the strength to never give up. There have been times that I thought I would never make it, and there were times that the feelings overwhelmed me so much that I attempted to take my own life, three times to be exact. One time I almost succeeded, they even called my family into say good bye to me. I remember hearing everyone crying and talking so upset, I remember it breaking my heart that they were so heart broken. I remember hearing the Dr. say that I may not make it her heart is not keeping up, my sister leaned over in my face and with anger and sadness said to me "Nadine, you have done it now! I literally came to and said "I'm not going anywhere" and started to wake up. I feel that because I said it out loud, god gave me the strength to not quit and he was not finished with me on this earth.

I would like to share a dream with you that I truly believe that God was preparing me for what I needed to do for him. For literally fifteen years, I had the reoccurring dream of leading others to freedom yelling at them to follow me, looking back yelling to come on and walking over all the dead souls that had given up on life and had stopped living because of sadness brought on by bad relationships, drugs and alcohol. I feel that a lot of people more than I could imagine suffer from lack of love for others and for themselves. The thing that scares me the most is that eventually we as a whole will become numb and that will be the end. We will no longer have trust or honesty in our marriages, families will not be whole.

That makes me so sad, I am going to everything in my power to make a difference. I truly believe all it takes all it takes is one person to love more than anyone has ever loved before. The kind of love that can get through to anyone, the kind of love Jesus had when he walked on this earth, we need more of that kind of love.

I feel that we need to retrain our view of things and how they should be, read the bible I have come to realize how interesting they are, the love stories that unfold. How the bible teaches us not to give upon love.

Girls start liking boys as early as elementary school, way before hormones come into play. Boys think girls are gross, next in junior high nature begins to take course. We pass the check yes or no notes, well now it's a text because at that age we just want to be able to say that we have a boyfriend or girlfriend. That's where it all begins the cycle of getting our hearts broken and bruised at such a young age. It amazes me even from my own experience I remember in 6th grade absolutely head over heels in love with this boy, and I look back today and he was so mean to me. He my best friends brother, he was a few years older than we were. This was back in the mid 80's when boys were not allowed to be at a girl's house unless a parent was home. They weren't allowed to be their rooms ever and if they were studying the door was open and the lights were on. They had to be back home by 8pm at the latest. That was a time when it was forbidden, cause daddy's put the fear of God in the boys who dated their daughters. A time when being a virgin was very common and was praised about. Sex education was taught in school we were advised to sustain, practice abstinence. I realize that there were sexual activities between teenagers from the beginning of time, I have read in history when a girl became a woman she was ready to marry and have babies. And back then in the olden days men were much older, took younger wives to raise large families to help with the farms. People lived very hard lives during those times, compared to now. Abuse existed and was ignored.

This was before the era of Women's Right's.

Jeannette Rankin's – 1848-1920—The suffrage leaders. The suffrage movement provided political training for some of early pioneer women. Back before this time men were allowed well not refrained from hitting their wives and children, severely abusing, no one ever said anything. People were very private during those times, Neighbors were few and far between, the only time people ever saw others were in town or during church.

Times never really changed to protect women and children from being abused until the 70's, over 100 years of abuse taking place, so many people minding their own and turning their heads, pretending no to see. Allowing someone to get hurt there's not a word I could use to describe the level of abuse that took place before DNA testing—restraining orders. Many times that women or children would reach out for help, and if it ever got out it became gossip instead of helping the victim, it would usually get talked about and taken out of perspective to the point the blame would be directed towards the one who was being abused, that behavior carried out up until the 80's well actually to this day as I am writing this.

During my time when I was growing up, God forbid anyone say that their parents were hurting them. Because if you were to go to someone you felt you could trust like at your school or church or even another family member. If they brought it to your parent's attention and let's say they weren't the ones hurting you, you would get into trouble for saying anything, because you were exaggerating or making it up. And if it were in fact your parent it would bring them negative attention, therefore cause you more negative attention. so then who you go to for help?

Now days if you speak loud or correct your kids and someone feels you are being inappropriate and would call child protective services. it has gone to the extreme. And without even taking a look into the situation they start investigating just for trying to teach our kids right from wrong.

Now in the present time I read and see on the news, Case after Case of not only men but women hurting babies sexually as young as seven months old. When I was in my early twenties when someone was sent to prison for child abuse they didn't make it out alive because inside people felt it was the ultimate crime. So they would deal with it themselves. It seems now there's so much of it being reported its out of control. Most of it is drug related. Now at 44 years old and have seen so much during my years on this earth. I have to say I am truly shaken by all that has surfaced. I know that I am not the only one in this day in time who is disturbed by what is going on in our world today. I have the strongest desire to talk about what I am seeing and make a statement that will wake everyone up. open their eyes stand up and fight. Fight for the respect and honor we all deserve. The have always said that women have the power to rule the world, quite frankly I agree. I need and want to teach on a higher level larger scale the tools that will allow women and children to walk away and never look back at any negative influence or energy that will take their innocence from them and taint their hearts.

Printed in the United States
By Bookmasters